CHEERLEADING

Written by

Piper Welsh

rourkeeducationalmedia.com

Scan for Related Titles
and Teacher Resources

www.rourkeeducationalmedia.com

PHOTO CREDITS: 1; © bikeriderlondon, 4; © Pavel Losevsky | Dreamstime.com, 5; © CHEN WS / Shutterstock.com, 6; © nojustice, 7; © Everett Collection, 8; © Aspen Photo / Shutterstock.com, 9; © Pavel L Photo and Video / Shutterstock.com, 10; © nullplus, 11; © bikeriderlondon, Moodboard, 12; © Khakimullin Aleksandr, 13; © Aspen Photo, 14; © RichVintage, 15; © Eric Broder Van Dyke, 16; © leezsnow, 17; © Andriy Popov, 18; © aceshot1 / Shutterstock.com, 19; © Shariff Che\' Lah | Dreamstime.com, 20; © Aspen Photo / Shutterstock.com, 21; © Aspen Photo / Shutterstock.com, 22; © Pavel L Photo and Video / Shutterstock.com

Editor: Jill Sherman

Cover Designer: Tara Raymo

Interior Designer: Cory Davis

Library of Congress PCN Data

Cheerleading / Piper Welsh
Fun Sports for Fitness
  ISBN 978-1-62169-857-9 (hardcover)
  ISBN 978-1-62169-752-7 (softcover)
  ISBN 978-1-62169-959-0 (ebook)
Library of Congress Control Number: 2013936462

Also Available as:

Rourke Educational Media
Printed in the United States of America,
North Mankato, Minnesota

Rourke
Educational Media

rourkeeducationalmedia.com

customerservice@rourkeeducationalmedia.com • PO Box 643328 Vero Beach, Florida 32964

Table of Contents

The Sport of Cheerleading. 4

Early Days of Cheerleading 7

Safety of the Sport 8

Jumps and Dances. 10

Sidelines and Cheers 14

Hand and Arm Positions 16

Cheerleading Stunts 18

Tumbling 20

Cheerleading Competitions 22

Glossary 23

Index 24

Websites to Visit 24

Show What You Know 24

The Sport Of Cheerleading

The first question many people ask is if cheerleading is a sport or an activity that supports other sporting events. Cheerleading has changed a lot over the years. Today it's known for athleticism, entertainment, and even student leadership. Both physical and mental skills are developed through cheerleading.

Competitive cheerleading requires great athleticism.

Ask any cheerleader and he or she will tell you it's a sport! The skill involved, the hours of training, and the high level of competition make cheerleading a demanding discipline that is much more than just an after-school activity.

Early Days of Cheerleading

Princeton University had the first cheerleaders in 1870. They would lead the crowd in chants, fight songs, and cheers. In the 1920s, women at the University of Minnesota added tumbling **routines**. Later, professional cheerleading squads were organized for the National Football League.

Since the 1970s, Pop Warner has recognized cheerleading and conducted many successful programs for young athletes in this fast-growing activity.

Safety of the Sport

Practice makes perfect. A careless mistake could result in injury.

Every cheerleading coach needs to create an environment where safety is the highest priority. In addition to its cheers and dance routines, cheerleading may include stunts that must be executed with great **precision**.

Many coaches have their teams sign a "Full-Value Contract," by which squad members agree to work together, to follow safety rules, and to practice positive teamwork.

To avoid injuries, each member of a cheerleading squad must be totally committed not only to his or her own safety, but also to the safety of every other member of the squad. Spotters help guide and teach stunts and tricks. These spotters are experienced cheerleaders who also make sure no one gets injured.

Jumps and Dances

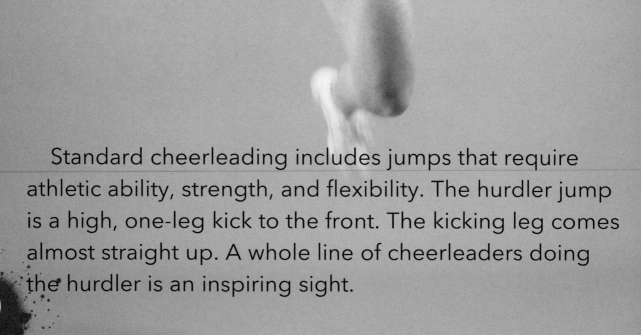

Standard cheerleading includes jumps that require athletic ability, strength, and flexibility. The hurdler jump is a high, one-leg kick to the front. The kicking leg comes almost straight up. A whole line of cheerleaders doing the hurdler is an inspiring sight.

The tuck is another cheerleading jump. In this **maneuver**, both knees are brought to the chest while the arms shoot out to the sides in a V shape. A key to any good jump is snapping into position and holding the pose for as long as possible.

It is vital that any cheerleading session or practice begins with a warm-up stretch. With all the jumping and dance, pulled muscles are a constant concern.

The herkie is a harder jump. Like the hurdler, it has a high, one-leg kick, but to the side instead of forward. The other leg is bent, with the knee facing the ground. Perhaps the hardest jump is the toe touch, with both legs lifting high and to the sides in an aerial split, and with the arms pointing in a wide, downward V.

Dance is becoming a major part of cheerleading. Many teams even hire professional **choreographers** to design routines. Hip-hop music has influenced dance steps in cheerleading, expanding the cultural horizon and creating new routines.

Sidelines and Cheers

Cheerleaders talk to the crowd using chants, cheers, and sidelines. The key to effective chants is to keep them simple and to make them **rhythmic**. Chants are designed both to motivate players and to excite spectators. If they're too complicated, they won't work.

Cheers have more content and deliver a specific message. Sidelines are short and repetitive. In competitions, sidelines are used between the musical stunting portion of a routine and the final cheers.

Hand and Arm Positions

There are several basic hand positions. The bucket is a palm-down fist with the thumb tucked under. The blade has all four fingers and thumb thrust straight ahead. The candlestick is a vertical fist with the palm facing out. The dagger is a fist with the heel of the hand and pinky facing forward. The knocker is a fist with the knuckles facing front.

Among the many arm positions are the T, with arms out, **parallel** to the ground. The high V has arms held up at a slight outward angle. A low V has arms down at a slightly outward angle. A diagonal has one arm in a high V and the other in a low V. An L has one arm straight up and the other straight out parallel to the ground.

Any arm position with bent elbows is called "broken." A broken T is a T with the elbows bent and the fists pointing toward each other in front of the chest.

Cheerleading requires precision and sharpness. Hand motions can't be sloppy, particularly the punches. The up punch has one fist on the hip while the other fires straight overhead. In a punch out or punch forward, both fists snap straight ahead at chest level.

A cross or front cross is carried out when one fist shoots out to the front across the chest while the other fist stays on the hip. These positions may be used in **combination** to create different kinds of routines and different types of cheers.

Cheerleaders' props include pom-poms, banners, scarves, or ribbons. Cheerleaders may also hold up signs or decorative boxes with team **insignia**.

Cheerleading Stunts

Stunts are the most exciting part of cheerleading. They can be breathtaking for both the audience and the participants. It's thrilling to pull off a great stunt in front of a big crowd.

The flyers are the top part of the stunt **structure**. They are the small, athletic squad members who rely on their teammates to ensure their safety from the moment they are launched until they're back in the arms of the catchers.

The bases are the bottom part of the stunt structure. They are the big, strong athletes who both throw and catch the flyers. Balance and strength are critical. Spotters are very important in stunts. They make sure flyers don't fall through the catchers and hit the ground.

The thigh stand or half stand, is one of the most basic stunts for new cheerleaders. Yet it requires strength and stability in the base and agility in the flyers.

Tumbling

A key part of cheerleading is tumbling. Those who are flexible and can dance make excellent tumblers. Gymnasts can be good cheerleaders because they practice many of the same moves. Grace, artistry, speed, and strength all make up tumbling at its best.

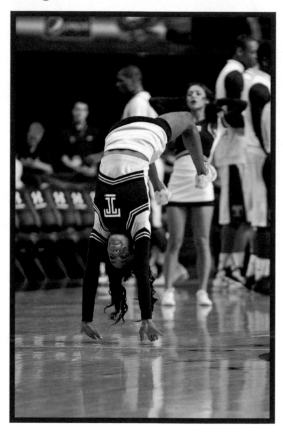

A cheerleading team may build many tumbling maneuvers into its routine. They include front and back rolls, handstands, cartwheels, round-offs, front walkovers, and back walkovers. With practice, any cheerleader can master these basics.

In addition to the basics, there are some challenging tumbles a squad may learn. These include the aerial cartwheel, front handspring, back handspring, round-off back handspring, and serial front and back handsprings.

Advanced tumbling skills include the triple combination of a round-off back handspring into a back tuck, a back somersault in the layout position, and a whipback somersault. These should be taught only by an expert instructor.

Serious cheerleading training focuses on power, balance, flexibility, and body fat reduction.

Cheerleading Competitions

Cheerleading has become as competitive as any sport around. There are currently hundreds of organized meets and competitions all around the country. Every year, teams from large, mid-size, and small schools go head to head for school pride and recognition.

Glossary

choreographers (kor-ee-OG-ruh-furz): people who create dance routines

combination (kom-bih-NAY-shun): the result of bringing together two or more elements

insignia (in-SIG-nee-ah): distinguishing signs

maneuver (mah-NOO-ver): a physical movement requiring skill or dexterity

parallel (PAR-uh-lel): being an equal distance apart at every point

precision (pree-SIZH-un): showing exactness in movement or action

rhythmic (RITH-mick): happening with regularity

routines (roo-TEENZ): detailed courses of action

structure (STRUCK-chur): something made of several parts held together a particular way

Index

athleticism   4

bases   19

catchers   18, 19

chants   7, 14

competitions   15, 22

dance(s)   8, 13, 20

flyers   18, 19

hand   16, 17

herkie   12

hip-hop   13

hurdler   10, 12

Pop Warner   7

routine(s)   7, 8, 13, 15, 17, 20

safety   8, 9, 18

sidelines   14, 15

spotters   9, 19

stunts   8, 9, 18, 19

toe touch   12

tuck   11, 21

tumbling   7, 20, 21

Websites to Visit

www.varsity.com

www.active.com/cheerleading

www.americancheerleader.com

Show What You Know

1. Why is it important to be safe while performing cheerleading stunts?

2. Is it necessary to be athletic to be a cheerleader? Why?

3. What is the difference between a cheer and a sideline?

4. When was cheerleading invented?

5. Can you name three jumps used in cheerleading?